Adjusting to Divorce®
The 8-Step Approach

Dr. Percy Ricketts

Adjusting to Divorce®
The 8-Step Approach

For information, contact:
Counseling & Empowerment Consulting Group
10031 Pines Boulevard, Suite 242
Pembroke Pines, FL 33024

The author has made every effort to eliminate typographical and
other errors that may appear in this book. Any inaccuracies or
errors are inadvertent and regrettable. The content of this book is
intended for general information only.

ISBN 13:978-0-692-19312-9

Images courtesy of Clipart.com and Canstockphoto.com

Printed in the United States of America

Adjusting to Divorce
The 8-Step Approach

A well-adjusted mom with her well-adjusted sons

When parents adjust well to separation or divorce, they are in a much better position to help their children.

Divorced parents at lunch with their children

It takes a high level of maturity for parents to recognize that, despite whatever differences may exist between them, they must put them aside and focus on the business of raising their children together.

When parents continue to work cooperatively and put their children's needs first, the children are more likely to adjust appropriately to the separation and divorce.

Boy having fun skating

Challenging situations occasionally arise in families. Still, parents should reassure their children that, whatever challenges they may face, they do have things under control, and they always have their children's best interests at heart.

Children shouldn't have to spend time worrying about complicated matters that pertain to their parents' separation or divorce. These are adult concerns that only the adults should have to worry about and find solutions for. Children should be allowed to be children and enjoy their lives.

Boy sad after he learns about his parents' divorce

One of the best ways that parents can tell if their children are adjusting well to separation or divorce is to pay close attention to their behavior. If drastic changes are observed, like sadness, preferring to be alone, or frequently expressing anger, these could be signs of poor adjustment. They may require further investigation and, at times, even intervention by trained professionals.

The 8-Step Approach

Well-adjusted boys

Because boys in our society are socialized not to express deep emotional feelings openly, they often suffer most when families separate or divorce. Having a plan in place to help all minor children adjust appropriately when significant changes occur in a family is a good goal for parents to consider.

Children of divorce with their friends

After a divorce, children should be encouraged to spend time with their friends and with members of their extended family. A good social support system is paramount in helping children adjust, especially following a major change like divorce.

Introduction

It's a very common story. Two people meet. They fall in love. And soon they decide they want to spend the rest of their lives together. They decide to get married. They plan a wedding. They invite their relatives and their closest friends. And they take lifelong vows.

Nothing is wrong with this story. However, there has been a trend in our society for decades that within eight to ten years of exchanging eternal vows, and even after having children, roughly half of all married Americans decide to divorce.

Divorce is a major stressor that affects millions of adults and children in our society. Every year, more than a million couples divorce in the United States, and more than a million children are affected (US Census Bureau 2006).

When marriages end, the consequences can be disastrous, especially for the children, many of whose lives are often affected forever. Indeed, the pain and trauma that divorce often brings sometimes go on to affect even those in subsequent generations. Children whose parents divorced are more likely to divorce as adults.

Despite the difficulties that separation and divorce often bring, many people whose marriages fail remarry within a few years. Studies show that second and subsequent marriages usually end much more quickly than first marriages. Yet within five to ten years, 80 percent of divorced men and 75 percent of divorced women have already remarried (National Fatherhood Initiative 2015).

Studies also affirm that decades after a marriage ends, some parents are still angry, and some might still be experiencing difficulties moving ahead with their lives. Even so, many remarry anyway, hoping perhaps that things might magically change.

To make matters even worse, although the breakup of a family can be very difficult, many parents soon realize that the divorce is not the end of their interactions with their ex-spouse as they may have initially hoped. Rather, because they have children together, they still must communicate with each other, and they must do so amicably. Quite often, this situation presents more challenges than parents anticipated.

Within a very short time after separating or divorcing, some individuals are faced with the harsh reality that co-parenting their children with someone they probably wish to avoid can indeed be very stressful. After all, they know only too well that they already have a history of finding it difficult to get along with each other for any sustained period.

Insofar as children are concerned, they are the ones who usually suffer the most when families break up. Depending on a variety of factors, children whose parents divorce are oftentimes at great risk for developing emotional, behavioral, and other problems, many of which will continue to affect them even when they become adults.

Studies on families confirm that children of divorce are more likely to perform poorly in school and to use drugs. They are more likely to be depressed and to engage in early sexual activity (National Fatherhood Initiative 2015). This is in strict contrast with many of their peers who live with parents who get along with each other.

Quite often, it is not the divorce itself that children say is most difficult for them. They are usually well aware that their parents have not been getting along, and they yearn for peace in the family. They usually implicate many factors as major stressors, including their parents' continued inability to resolve conflicts immediately and appropriately when they arise.

Additionally, many children say their parents continuously involve them in their disagreements, and some even expect them to take sides. Separation and divorce are usually traumatic for children. However, some children feel relieved when their parents finally decide to stop the fighting by living separately.

One of the most significant stressors for many children is when their parents get involved in new relationships soon after the family breaks up, and they have to deal with stepparents. Some children view separation as a temporary measure that their parents adopted to stop fighting. Therefore, some children might look forward to a time when family members are back together again in the same home. When the separation becomes permanent and the reality of a divorce sinks in, some children are simply devastated.

Many children regard these as some of the main factors that affect them when families break up. They view them not only as causing prolonged trauma and pain, but also as spilling over into other areas of their lives, arresting their overall development, and making it far more difficult for them to adjust to other important situations.

Despite the numerous challenges that parents and children often face following divorce, there are simple steps that parents can take that can help make adjusting to this life-altering process less painful and less traumatic for everyone. Eight of these steps are outlined in this volume.

Teenage children of divorce strolling together

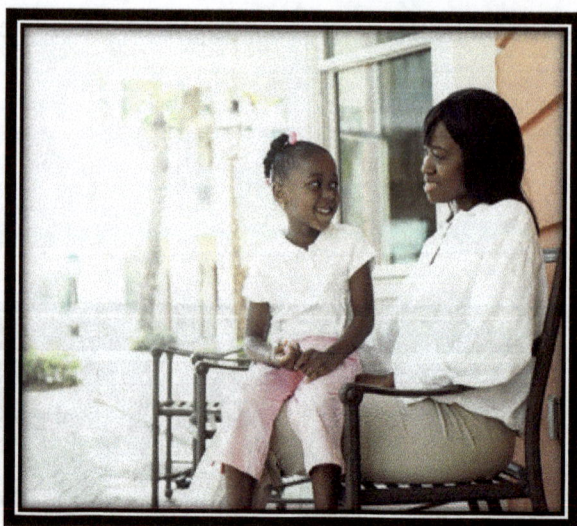

An African American mother with her daughter

Separation, divorce, and remarriage rates are significant concerns in the United States, especially among minority groups. Data shows that black women file for divorce more frequently than their white counterparts and that they are less eager to remarry as well (National Fatherhood Initiative 2015).

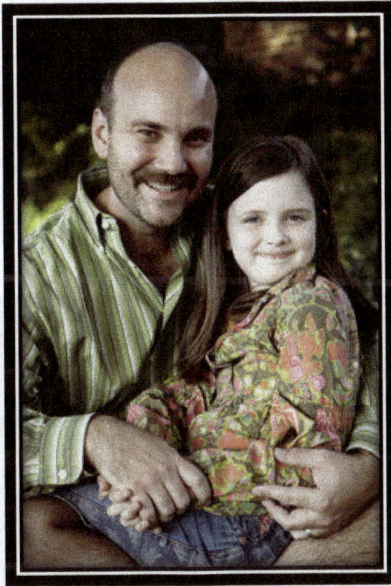

A father with his daughter after his divorce

The presence of fathers and their consistent involvement in their children's lives are essential ingredients for the children's overall healthy development. Even so, the absence of fathers continues to be a major concern in the United States, especially in minority households.

10

According to *Father Facts 7* (National Fatherhood Initiative 2015), America leads the world in number of households that are without fathers.

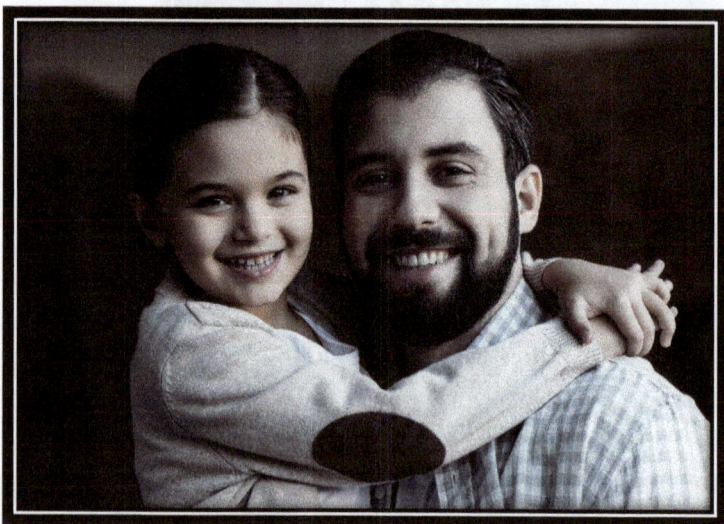

A father with his daughter

**Parents expressing their disagreements in
the presence of their teenage daughter**

If parents continue to disagree with each other

after they separate or divorce, it makes it much harder

for their children to adjust.

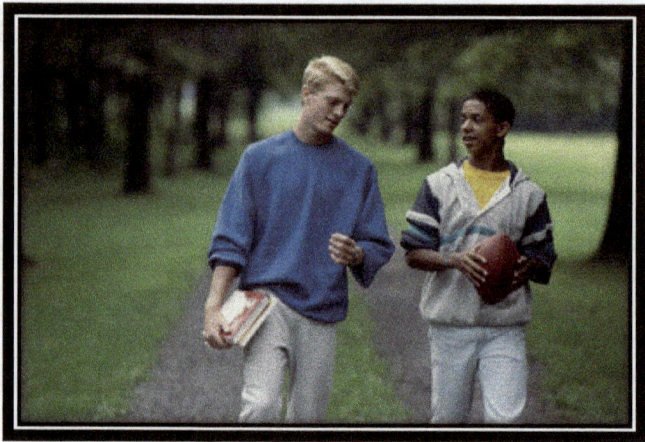

Well-adjusted high school boys. Boys are usually more affected by divorce than girls are.

A child's ability to adjust to divorce depends on many factors. These include his or her age at the time of the divorce, the time of year the divorce takes place, whether other significant events are occurring while the divorce is in progress, the reason for the divorce, and how the parents interact with each other and with the child while the divorce is in progress and especially after it is final.

A father with his children after his divorce

Step #1

Get Divorce Education for Yourself and Your Children

Children in a divorce education class

In many jurisdictions in the United States, adults who are seeking a divorce are required to enroll in family stabilization programs before their divorce can be finalized in the courts.

In some areas, it is mandatory for children of divorce to take special education classes as well. Even so, parents are sometimes reluctant to enroll themselves or their children in these types of programs. Many parents and children never receive the help they could use after their families break up.

Many of those who do get assistance attest to the helpful nature of divorce education programs for themselves and their children. It is highly recommended, therefore, that when contemplating a separation or divorce, parents consider enrolling themselves and their children in these special programs.

Through these programs, parents learn a great deal about divorce and how it can affect them and steps they can take to adjust appropriately. They are made aware, for example, of the legal and emotional aspects of divorce and how their attitudes and behavior could affect them and their children.

Parents learn about their expected roles and their obligations to their children and their ex-spouses after the family's breakup. They also learn how their choices and decisions can affect their welfare and that of their children.

Many parents also learn how to address and even avoid important pitfalls that sometimes emerge before, during, and after a divorce. Additionally, and perhaps even more importantly, they learn effective strategies that they can use to help make adjusting to divorce much easier for themselves and their children.

One of the most important lessons that many parents learn in divorce education classes, however, is why it is necessary for them to talk to their children about the divorce and why it is important for the conversation to take place before one parent decides to move out of the home. Parents are given effective ways to have that very important conversation about the separation or divorce with their children.

Before they divorce, parents are often unaware of the various ways that this life changer can affect them and their children. Indeed, some parents are even unaware of where they can get help when challenging situations emerge after they divorce.

Parents, especially those who are divorcing for the first time, need to become more aware that, when it comes to children, the divorce does not take place when the final decree is granted by the courts. Rather, it really happens on the day that one parent physically leaves the home to reside elsewhere. Many children, therefore, start to experience the loss from the family breakup long before their parents suspect that they could use some help.

From this standpoint, when a parent leaves the home without saying anything to his or her children or when he or she decides to wait until the divorce is final in the courts to talk to them, some damage can indeed be inflicted. Despite this knowledge, however, many parents separate for several years without having any conversation with their children.

Many individuals who are now adults say they have no knowledge of any discussion ever taking place when their parents separated. Parents' failure to converse with their children about this life-altering process can result in further confusion in the children's lives. It leads some children to assume wrongfully that their parents avoided the subject because they (the children) did something wrong.

Other children develop the idea that because they might have caused the divorce, the parent who leaves might stop loving them or that he or she might abandon them after leaving the home. For years, therefore, some children live with the idea that it is their job to get their parents back together.

Unless parents tell children otherwise, some of them could continue to assume for a very long time that they were the cause of their parents' divorce. This idea causes some children to feel that because the divorce was their fault, it is their job to find creative ways to reunite their parents and to put the family back together.

In their attempts to reunite their parents following a separation or divorce, children use various strategies. Some make themselves sick so both parents have to take them to the doctor. Some children tell lies, or they steal things that they don't need. Other children may try to break up new relationships in which their parents are involved. When their efforts to reunite their parents fail, they may continue to blame themselves and to feel guilty for something they did not do and simply

could not have done.

A father leaving home

To help children adjust well to separation or divorce, both parents should talk to them together before one parent leaves the home.

How can parents prevent their children from getting the wrong idea about their decision to divorce? What matters are important for parents to cover in a conversation with their children about this very important subject?

Conversations with children and adults who have been in separation and divorce situations confirm that there are some very important points that should be covered in discussions with children about these matters. These include the following:

1. The parents should get together first and rehearse what they will say to their children about the divorce.

2. Mom, Dad, and all the children should be present at the meeting.

3. Parents should be willing to answer all questions that the children have, and they should be prepared to deal with whatever emotions may arise.

4. In order to confirm that the decision to divorce was made by both parents, the word *we* should be used very often in the conversation.

5. There should be no "side conversations" with individual children before or after the meeting. Neither should there be any negative discussion by one parent about the other.

6. Once the parents decide when they will have the conversation with the children, the children should be informed immediately.

7. The discussion should take place as scheduled.

8. The children should be told that they will have the opportunity to ask as many questions as they wish, and they should be assured that all their questions will be answered.

9. The parents should assure the children that they do not have to worry because the parents will continue to work together to ensure that the transition after the divorce is not difficult and that their needs are still met.

10. The children should be told that both parents have been experiencing significant problems while they have been living together. (Usually the children are already well aware of this.)

11. The children should be told that both parents tried to make things better, but they have not been able to do so.

12. The children should be told that their parents are very sad that they have been unable to get along better with each other and that they have not been able to keep the family together.

13. The parents should tell the children that because things have not been improving, they have both decided that it is better if they live in separate homes.

14. The children should be told that although the parents will be living separately, they will still continue to love them and care for them.

15. The children should be told that they will continue to spend time with both parents.

16. Both parents should emphasize that the decision to separate or to divorce is not impulsive and that they decided to separate only after all efforts to improve the marriage failed.

17. The children should be told that the relationship between parents is different from the relationship between parents and children. Therefore, while the relationship between the parents might have changed, the relationship between each parent and each child has not changed and will not change.

18. The children should be told that the decision to separate was not because of anything they (the children) did or didn't do. Therefore, the divorce is not their fault.

19. The children should be told that there is nothing they can do to change their parents' minds about separating or divorcing and that they should not try to get them back together.

20. The children should be assured that the details regarding when they will spend time with each parent have been worked out, and both parents agree with the arrangements. They should then be told what the arrangements are.

Parents should try to include other points in the conversation that they believe might be beneficial to the children, based on their unique family situation. Many adults whose parents divorced consistently list the following among major fears and concerns that they had: uncertainty if their parents would continue to love

27

and care for them, feeling that the separation or the divorce was their fault, and believing that it was their role to try to get their parents back together.

Studies confirm that of every four children whose families divorce, at least one child feels abandoned by one parent (usually the one who left) (National Fatherhood Initiative 2015). Other studies reveal that children of divorce consistently list dealing with stepfamilies as one of the biggest challenges they ever faced (National Fatherhood Initiative 2015).

Despite these concerns, however, fewer people in the United States are now in first marriages than in second marriages and other types of blended family arrangements. Additionally, based on current trends, it is predicted that many of today's children should expect to spend a significant portion of their childhood in families that are no longer intact or in families in which at least one parent remains angry because of divorce concerns (National Fatherhood Initiative 2015).

Divorce programs for children are usually conducted in groups based on the children's age. They are usually supportive in nature, and they provide numerous opportunities for children to interact with each other and learn how to express their feelings about the divorce openly and appropriately.

Through divorce education groups, children learn what divorce means. They also learn how their lives could change when their families break up and that, just like them, other children are facing similar challenges and coping well. This gives the children hope that whatever difficulties may arise because of the divorce, they, too, can overcome them.

The groups also give children the opportunity to learn numerous valuable skills from each other, which they can use in various situations that emerge following divorce. These skills are very important to many children because they can use them on their own to make their adjustment to the divorce easier.

Parents should make every effort to research divorce education programs in their communities. Many of these programs can address whatever unique challenges their children are experiencing following their decision to divorce.

Parents should also try to remember that divorce is a significant loss in the lives of their children. It could very well be the first major loss that they ever experienced. Moreover, as with any other significant loss, children do go through a grieving process that is not only new, but also often very difficult for them.

Many children have neither the experience nor an adequate vocabulary to express feelings of loss appropriately. Also, because some parents avoid talking to their children about separation and divorce, and because they often assume that their children are coping much better than they are, many children are denied the help they could use to cope more effectively with one of the biggest traumas they might ever face.

Parents should make sure that they do not use education programs as a substitute for taking the time to talk with their children about separation and divorce. In fact, even in areas where divorce education programs might not exist or those where they might not be mandatory, it is still beneficial for parents to find other means to educate themselves and their children on this very important subject. When parents are informed, they put themselves in much better positions to help themselves and to continue to help their children.

Children in a divorce education class

All children have the right not just to have both parents present and actively involved in their lives, but also to have the best parents who love them, continuously guide them, and care for them.

**Parents who still have a good relationship
after they divorce**

Children do much better overall when their
parents maintain good relationships and when they
continue to co-parent appropriately after they separate
or divorce.

Step #2

Understand Your New Role as a Divorced Co-Parent

Parents fighting in their son's presence

When parents fight with each other often, especially in their children's presence, it can be very difficult for the children to maintain good emotional health.

35

Parents' roles and their relationships with their children can change in unique ways after they separate or divorce. The children no longer have the comfort of having both parents living together in the same home, and the situation gets even more complicated when the reality of being two single parents, often with different ideas about child-rearing, begins to sink in.

Depending on numerous factors, including the children's ages at the time of the divorce, how the divorce process is handled by the parents and the children, whether the parents talk to their children about the divorce and what is discussed, and how and when stepfamilies emerge, the situation can become very problematic.

Despite the problems that may arise, however, and regardless of how families might change, there are certain responsibilities that both parents will still have. Chief among these responsibilities is continuing to meet their children's basic needs.

While parents are married, there is oftentimes role confusion. This sometimes leads to frequent disagreements and failure to meet the children's needs. This was certainly not the case in previous decades, however, when mothers' work was essentially confined to the home, and fathers were expected to be sole breadwinners who worked outside it.

Numerous changes over the years have resulted in many mothers making their mark alongside men in the workplace. This trend, along with what some see as a drastic change in women's attitudes, has apparently had major influences on children's lives. It is also often implicated among factors said to be responsible for changes in the ways families are structured today and how they function.

Other important family concerns in today's society include views some postmodern women have about families, how they view fathers and their roles, and the erroneous ideas that some seem to embrace regarding whether fathers are even as essential as many studies consistently suggest.

Despite much evidence to the contrary, some popular ideas suggest that mothers can raise children successfully alone, that fathers are not as necessary as they were once thought, and that families are better off without them.

Indeed, many mothers now feel that because they are able to provide monetarily for themselves and their children, fathers are unnecessary following reproduction. Still, research on families consistently tells a different story.

Today, 24 million children in the United States live in homes without fathers. Almost 20 million live in single parent homes, usually with a single mother. The statistics on children who are raised without fathers are very disturbing. The data suggests that children who are raised in homes where the father is absent are more likely to do poorly in school, and they are more likely to be abused. These children are also more likely to develop behavioral problems and end up in jail. They are more likely to engage in early sexual activity, and girls are more likely to become teenage mothers. They are more likely to use drugs, and they are more likely to run away from home (National Fatherhood Initiative 2015).

These findings confirm that a father's involvement is crucial to children's positive development. Yet the number of families in the United States without fathers remains a major social concern that is not receiving the attention it aptly deserves.

Despite the numerous challenges that many fathers face, mothers are undoubtedly not the only ones responsible for all society's ills. In fact, based on what we now know about fathers' importance in families, it is abundantly clear that many fathers could work much harder to maintain their involvement in their children's lives.

Many mothers could also make it easier for fathers to remain involved in their children's lives. It is time for some mothers to discard the idea of denying children their right to have their fathers involved in their lives because when fathers are absent, children are at risk for numerous disadvantages. The ideas that some mothers have about parenting and the father's involvement and the decisions they make in that regard are hurting their own children.

Fathers should also recognize that their presence in their children's lives is paramount. Regardless of their marital status, many mothers and fathers in our society need to take their roles in their children's lives more seriously.

Primarily because of the numerous changes that have been taking place over the years in our society, there has also been a gradual blending of male-female roles. This blending appears to be confusing some parents, specifically in terms of what their individual roles should be in their children's lives, especially after they divorce. Some parents are also confused about the basic needs of their children that they need to meet consistently. Regardless of a parent's marital status, he or she is still obligated to provide at least eight basic needs for his or her children. These needs are:

1. Food

2. Clothing

3. Shelter

4. Education

5. Health care

6. Love

7. Guidance

8. Safety

In order to ensure that their children's needs are met consistently following divorce, parents usually draw up legally binding support orders based on certain guidelines. Among other stipulations, these guidelines often determine who pays for what, when, to whom, how much, and for how long.

Traditionally, there has been a trend giving mothers custody of minor children while fathers make support payments. In recent times, however, this trend has been changing. Many fathers are now gaining equal access to their children following divorce, and there are also many fathers who have sole custody of their children. Many mothers are also making support payments for their children—a role that historically was ascribed mainly to fathers.

The importance of parents making support payments cannot be overstated. Still, getting parents to do so consistently poses a major challenge for some families. When parents fail to make support payments, or when they are inept in their other roles, it usually results in undue hardship for their children, and it can cause significant disruption in their lives.

Studies confirm that when fathers continue to care for their children financially following divorce and when they make support payments promptly, they have much closer relationships with their children. Other studies show that when children receive regular support payments from their fathers and when their fathers stay involved in their lives, they do much better overall (National Fatherhood Initiative 2015).

Following divorce, parents are expected to continue spending time with their children. We now know that it is not just the quality of the time that is important when it comes to children's well-being. Rather, especially when children are young, the quantity of time that parents spend with them on a consistent basis is what is really important.

In many jurisdictions, parents are required to present very detailed time-sharing and co-parenting plans to the courts before their divorces can be finalized. Among the many considerations that these plans must address are the various tasks that each parent will perform, when they will perform them, how much time the children will spend with each parent, and what being with them will entail.

The plans should also consider other factors including the children's weekly living arrangements and what happens during vacations, on major holidays, and even on birthdays. Time-sharing and co-parenting plans should be flexible enough to meet the children's needs as they go from one stage of development to another.

Parents find it beneficial when they make special efforts to understand what their obligations and roles should be, specifically in terms of caring for their children after their divorce. By doing so, and by consistently adhering to what is required of them, many of the conflicts that often arise following divorce can be avoided. Some of these conflicts have negative effects on parents and on their children's ability to adjust appropriately to separation and divorce.

When parents neglect to provide adequately for their children, they can be subject to legal repercussions. Many of these matters pertaining to parents' roles following divorce, as well as others that often result in post-divorce conflicts, are addressed in detail in divorce education programs.

Happy children of divorce

A father and his children after his divorce

Despite conversations to the contrary, studies consistently confirm the numerous benefits to children when both their adoptive or biological parents are present and involved in their lives.

A mom spending time with her children after divorce

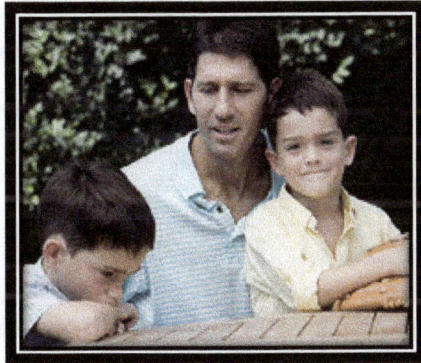

A dad spending time with his children after divorce

Both moms and dads should spend time with their children frequently after a divorce.

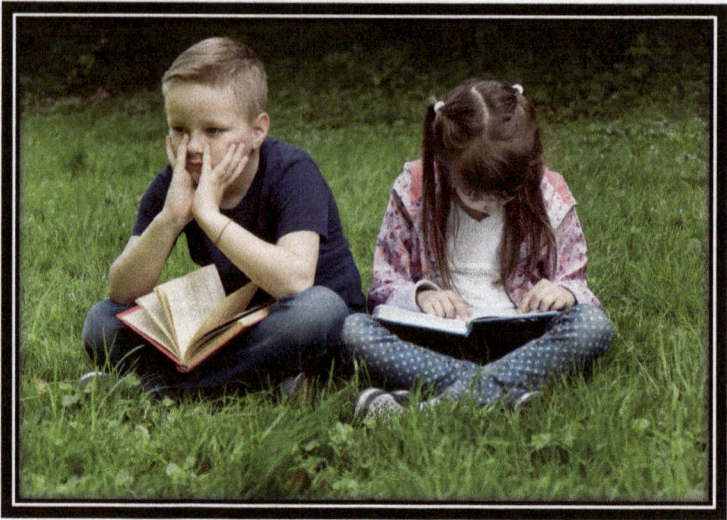

Boy not doing well after his parents divorce

After a divorce, sometimes children tend to behave one way when they are with their parents and a totally different way, when they are not with them. This often makes the parents feel that they are adjusting very well to the divorce, when in fact, it might not be the case.

Step #3

Model Good Behavior at All Times

Parents behaving badly.

Children learn from their parents' behavior. When parents consistently display positive behaviors, their children are more likely to do so as well. When they display negative behaviors, the children are also more likely to do likewise.

One major concern following divorce is that many parents find it difficult to put their differences aside so they can model good behavior for their children. When parents model good behavior, their children learn how to conduct themselves appropriately in various situations. In fact, many children report that it is neither the separation nor the divorce that hurts them the most, but rather, it is the constant fighting in which their parents continue to engage, sometimes even years after they divorce.

Some parents bad-mouth each other. They call each other names. They use their children as messengers and spies. They get their children involved in their battles, and they generally conduct themselves in a negative manner that makes it very difficult for everyone to adjust to the divorce and move forward appropriately with their lives.

Divorce can be very difficult. And the numerous difficulties that parents encounter, along with the wide range of emotions they often experience, can cause them to display inappropriate behavior that is not good for their children to observe at all.

Even so, parents are responsible for managing their emotions in order to prevent their children from seeing them behaving inappropriately. Regardless of the difficulties parents may encounter, and despite whatever negative emotions they might experience as a result of their decision to divorce, they should still try very hard to be on good terms with each other for their children's sake.

Many parents find it very difficult to continue to work together to meet their children's needs effectively after the divorce, especially if the process was traumatic and painful. Still, when parents find it difficult to work together to meet their children's needs, it can complicate and lengthen the adjustment process, especially for the children.

Parents should try to remember that just as the divorce does not mean that their relationships with their children have ended, neither does it signify an end to their relationships with their children's other parent. There will be many occasions on which parents will have to interact with each other for their children's benefit, even after the children become adults. Both parents are still expected to be present at parent-teacher conferences, sporting events, and other extracurricular activities in which their children are involved; at graduations and weddings; in emergency room situations; at award ceremonies and birthday parties; at the births of grandchildren; and at numerous other important events. How parents choose to behave when they attend those activities and how well they interact with each other and with their children can have a significant influence on their own recovery from the divorce and their children's.

Children model their parents' behaviors, even if the behaviors are negative. Therefore, parents should consider how their actions and interactions with each other can affect their children.

Parents make many important decisions that can be beneficial to their children's development. They move to "good" neighborhoods. They send their children to the "right" schools, and they provide for them very well, ensuring they have access to many novelties to which they themselves might not have been fortunate enough to be exposed as children.

Still, when parents make decisions that can have a positive influence on their children's development but then treat each other terribly, any gains that were possible from those decisions are often lost or significantly diminished.

Years, sometimes even decades, after their divorce, some parents still experience significant difficulties in their interactions with each other. Some of these individuals are also aware that they have not yet fully recovered from the divorce, and they know their children are still being affected negatively by their behavior. Yet they continue to traumatize themselves and their children by not getting the help they need to display more prosocial behavior.

Many adults whose parents divorced when they were children now affirm that they could have used some help, especially during the period immediately after the decision was made to break up their families. They indicate that they continued to struggle with divorce-related concerns because their parents did not get them the help they needed.

Parents who find they are still struggling with divorce-related concerns that may have a negative effect on their or their children's well-being should consider getting help from trained professionals. Even if their children appear to be adjusting well, they should still consider getting help for them. Quite often, children are not adjusting well, but they do not tell either parent, for fear that they could upset them.

Domestic violence is another major concern following divorce. Situations can become violent when parents remain angry following divorce, and they receive no help to manage their emotions appropriately. Parents should be aware that domestic violence is a very serious issue in our society, and the consequences can be very severe. Once an individual allows him- or herself to react while he or she is angry, the outcome is often unpredictable, but it is usually negative.

Available statistics suggest that the incidence of domestic violence has been increasing over the years and that it is a matter that merits a great deal more attention. Although there are some women who are abusive toward men, women in our society are disproportionately affected by domestic violence.

Data suggests that a husband or boyfriend beats a woman every fifteen seconds in the United States and that about three women are killed every day. Other studies indicate that at least one out of every four women will experience some type of domestic violence situation (CDC.gov).

Many individuals need to develop better conflict resolution skills to enable them to display greater self-control when challenging situations arise in their relationships.

An upset father

Through counseling, individuals learn effective self-control skills that they can use in their relationships.

Parents behaving badly

While many parents try their hardest to behave appropriately, to get along well with each other, and to do what's best for their children after they separate or divorce, others find it difficult to do so.

The potential for abuse and domestic violence continues to be a matter of grave concern in many families, especially after separation or divorce.

62

A girl with her mother after the divorce

When parents interact lovingly with their children and with each other, the children are more likely to do well overall, whether the parents live together or not.

Step #4

Make Full Use of Community Resources

Parents are expected to continue working together to co-parent their children following divorce. Still, primarily because some parents have a history of not working well together, this expectation often results in significant difficulties for them.

The emotional, financial, and other adjustments that many parents must make following divorce can make the situation even more difficult. In many cases, individuals find that the divorce might have solved some old problems, but it also creates new and more challenging ones that they may not have anticipated.

Many parents report that following their divorce, they often feel alone, isolated, confused, and overwhelmed and don't know where to turn for help. To make matters even worse, friends and relatives are not always as supportive as they usually are or were expected to be. Some family members may start blaming individuals for the divorce, and they may even start to mistreat their once-beloved family member.

Some friends and relatives take sides. They avoid one individual, or they treat him or her unfairly. Others get tired of listening to divorce-related concerns at a time when a loyal friend might have needed them the most.

Some friends who are still married might show very clearly that they do not like to be around single or divorced people. They may perceive them as a threat to their own relationships, or they may feel that their goals and agendas have now changed, and they are no longer consistent with their own as married couples.

Some friends who are still married may prefer that their spouses no longer spend as much time as they once did with a newly divorced person. Regardless of how close they used to be, following their divorce, people are sometimes perceived as bitter, revengeful, and bad for the stability of surviving marriages.

All these factors can make the life of a newly divorced person very difficult, and sometimes they are not sure to whom they can turn for useful advice or much-desired support. Fortunately, help is available, and there are numerous resources that parents can access that can make their lives less complicated and their adjustment to the divorce far less stressful.

In order to make full use of those resources, however, parents should first try to assess what their immediate and long-term needs are and what resources they may require to help meet these needs. Three important resources that many parents find necessary following a separation or divorce are:

1. Financial
2. Legal
3. Counseling

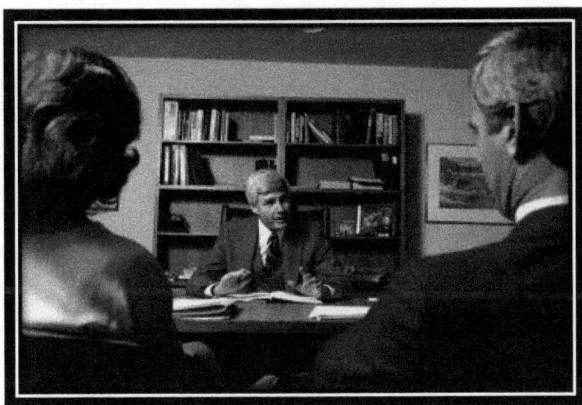

A family in mediation.

Mediation can be a great resource for many parents.

Numerous resources are available to help parents and their children cope appropriately with separation and divorce. Local libraries, for example, have books and a wide variety of movies that parents can borrow. Whether parents are contemplating separation or divorce, they are going through the process, or the process has already ended, they can benefit from identifying available resources in their communities and making full use of them.

Financial

Two incomes can usually do far more than one in family settings. Therefore, strictly from a financial perspective, it can be much cheaper and more advantageous for both parents live together in the same home and share financial and other resources as they co-parent their children.

It can be extremely difficult, however, when one parent is raising a child alone from the start, or when, for example, in the case of divorce, there is a drastic change from a two-parent household to a single-parent one. Following the divorce, one income replaces two.

This can create significant adjustment problems for many parents, specifically because they have grown accustomed to life in a dual-income household.

Financial concerns do rank very high among the challenges that parents face after a divorce. Additionally, soon after divorcing, some parents realize how difficult resolving divorce-related financial challenges can be. Even attempts to secure secondary employment that would allow them to earn extra income can be very challenging at times.

In many cases, even if extra work is available, parents find that the opportunity is not without major disadvantages. Extra hours working also mean more time away from their children, which can result in supervision problems and additional physical and financial stress.

Physical and financial stress are major factors in many post-divorce families—families that are easily further disrupted—at a time when they are already adjusting to a new life. If not managed well, stress often leads to other, more significant health concerns.

Legal

The fact that many parents find it so difficult to resolve their differences amicably before a separation or divorce occurs makes things even more difficult following the breaking of the emotional bonds they once shared. The advent of an emotionally charged situation like divorce often poses other unanticipated challenges for parents as well, which makes legal resources necessary at times.

Divorce also cannot take place without the use of the legal system. Hence, although some parents prepare for their divorce on their own (pro se), the need for consultation with legal personnel in many situations cannot be overemphasized. This consultation is even more important in the following situations:

1. When a couple has been married for several years.

2. When minor children are involved.

3. When couples have acquired significant assets during the marriage.

4. When there are major disagreements or when other important factors are involved.

Whether parents prepare their divorce documents on their own or use the services of legal professionals, the unavoidable involvement of the legal system means they should be aware of many aspects of this most important resource. Some parents try to avoid using legal resources in order to save money. Many soon discover, however, that this can be a very unwise and even expensive decision.

Numerous difficulties can arise when individuals with limited knowledge of the law choose to interpret and complete complex documents on their own. Unexpected difficulties can also arise when individuals try to make very important decisions that could have legal consequences without consulting trained and licensed legal professionals.

In many cases, parents realize that any savings they might have initially expected cannot compensate for the major mistakes that are sometimes inevitable. Parents should think very seriously about their approaches and about the decisions they make regarding the use of legal resources in their divorce.

Parents usually do not have much knowledge about the possible challenges they could face once their divorce is final either. Nor do they usually know where they can get appropriate help or when they should get professionals involved. Furthermore, some parents have a tendency to create a big mess first, then try to get professionals to help clean it up for them.

Even before parents decide to separate, they might find it beneficial to consult with legal professionals. This can help ensure that they understand what their rights are and how to proceed appropriately.

Even when experienced professionals are involved, divorce can be very difficult for many parents. When parents try to take on the additional task of navigating the legal system on their own, especially when their situation is already complicated and their understanding of the law is limited, it could make their situation more overwhelming unnecessarily.

Owing to inappropriate use of available resources or failure to use them, some individuals find themselves facing innumerable challenges, sometimes even years after their divorce is final. Many of these challenges could have been avoided, and they can inhibit parents' effectiveness in their expected roles after they divorce. They can also affect children's ability to adjust appropriately to divorce and the amount

of time it takes them to adjust as well.

A team of attorneys discussing a case before trial.

Family law attorneys are well versed in legal

proceedings. They are willing to help their clients with

challenging and complex legal matters.

Counseling

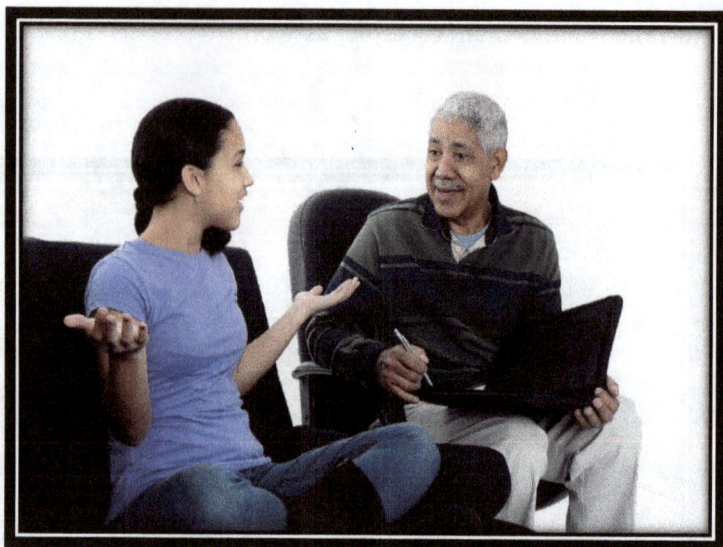

A girl with her therapist after her parents separated.

Counseling is a very important resource that many parents and children find useful, especially in the difficult times that sometimes arise after a separation or divorce.

77

A boy in individual counseling with his therapist after his parents divorce.

With professional assistance, many children learn new skills that they can use to help themselves adjust appropriately to the difficult and life-altering processes of separation and divorce.

Even in good times, counseling can be a most valuable resource for many individuals and their families. It is also one that is widely available in many communities in the United States. Yet evidence suggests that many parents are not making full use of this very important resource. Counseling can provide numerous benefits to parents and children during the divorce and, especially, immediately afterward.

Studies confirm that various barriers prevent many parents from accessing counseling. Quite often, parents wait until situations get worse or there is a crisis before they seek help for themselves or their children.

Parents should be mindful, however, that many concerns can be resolved with early intervention. Likewise, concerns that receive little or no attention can be difficult to resolve, and they can have undesirable outcomes.

It is important for parents to recognize that many difficulties may be involved when working on divorce-related concerns with children. For one thing, some children will not be willing to discuss family concerns openly because it might involve talking negatively about their parents. Children love both their parents dearly, and they do not like to be placed in positions that might involve speaking negatively about them.

Quite often, even when children are sent for counseling, because their parents have told them not to talk to strangers, they might not be willing to talk about how their lives are being affected by their parents' decisions or actions until they establish a good rapport with a counselor and various techniques are used to help them open up.

Because many children never raise questions about the divorce, some parents have the tendency to avoid the subject also. Other parents assume incorrectly that their children have been adjusting well because they might still be performing well in school and might not seem distressed.

The reality, however, is that children can be performing well academically, and they might not be showing obvious signs of distress. That does not necessarily mean that they are not experiencing extreme difficulties or that they are adjusting well to a major change like divorce.

Many children learn to hide their true feelings about the divorce from their parents very well. Therefore, parents should ensure that they are making sound evaluations of their children's behavior. They should talk to them about the divorce and look for inconsistencies and major changes in their behavior. These could signify adjustment difficulties, and help might indeed be needed.

In our society, people receive a great deal of help and support following the death of a loved one. Yet when another major loss like divorce occurs in a family, there is often no dialogue, or there is a great deal of animosity and bad-mouthing that can make things much worse.

Studies show that some children find divorce so difficult that they sometimes cope better with a parent's death than they do with divorce. Therefore, following divorce, it is very important that parents do not overlook the value of counseling, especially for their children.

If parents realized the numerous difficulties that their children can encounter when they are adjusting to divorce, they would probably take a more proactive approach toward ensuring that they receive help early in the divorce process.

Some children worry needlessly because they do not fully understand what divorce means, and they are not sure if their parents will continue to love them and care for them once the divorce is final. When children get the help they need, however, it is possible for them to develop a better understanding of what to expect while the divorce is occurring and afterward. They can also learn appropriate and effective coping skills they can use to help themselves and ways to avoid some of the challenges and crises they can encounter as they go through this very difficult process.

Various types of counseling services are available that parents can use to help themselves and their children. It is also important for parents to remember that it might not be in their best interest to wait until problems seem to be getting worse or there is a crisis before they decide to seek help.

If there is a crisis, however, special mental health units are available in many locations, and they will respond very quickly in certain situations. They will either make home visits to help families or provide helpful information via telephone, which many families can utilize immediately.

There are also community mental health centers in many areas of the United States. These types of organizations provide counseling, case management, and other related services to individuals who meet certain criteria. Perhaps even more importantly, because they are usually classified as not-for-profits and they receive funding from various sources, services are provided either for a nominal fee or at no cost to those who seek help.

Various religious organizations also provide counseling services. These services are usually provided at no cost, or clients can make a voluntary donation. Many religious educators are trained counselors who can help parents with the various challenges they encounter. Religious advisers have the added advantage of providing prayer and meditation for their clients, which many individuals find comforting during challenging times.

Parents can also utilize the services of various types of private mental health professionals. Private mental health professionals comprise a very diverse group. Nevertheless, they must meet certain state criteria and possess the specific licensing credentials that are essential for independent practice.

Some private mental health professionals specialize in counseling adults with divorce-related concerns, while others specialize in counseling the children of divorce and their families. Those in private practice may accept payments in cash only. However, they often have sliding fee scales, or they might be willing to work out special payment arrangements to help those facing financial challenges.

Other practitioners accept various types of private health insurance plans—health maintenance organizations (HMOs), preferred provider organizations (PPOs), or point of service (POS) plans. Employers may also provide access to job-based employee assistance programs (EAPs). EAPs usually provide an employee and his or her family members with brief counseling sessions to help resolve problems that could affect the employee's job performance.

Depending on the features of a particular plan, EAP sessions are usually available at no cost to the employees or to their family members. If more sessions are needed after EAP benefits are exhausted, health insurance benefits can then be used for continuation of care.

Many public schools have divorce support groups, and these can be an important resource for parents to get help for their children following a divorce. These special groups can play a vital role in helping children express their feelings about divorce with their peers in the presence of trained school counselors.

Where they are available, school-based support groups show children that others just like them are coping with similar challenges, and they are doing well. This gives them hope that they, too, can adjust well. Additionally, because other children are willing to express their feelings about their parents' divorce openly, it helps remove some of the stigma, shame, blame, and guilt that children often associate with divorce.

Many counselors share the belief that following a major loss like divorce, it is better to receive some help than no help at all. Therefore, because some children receive no help from their parents in adjusting to the divorce, school-based assistance with the guidance of trained counselors can prove to be very beneficial.

Clearly, parents have numerous options when it comes to getting help for themselves and for their children following divorce. They are encouraged to choose those options they feel might best meet their unique needs and the needs of their children.

Regardless of the approaches parents decide to utilize when it comes to counseling, however, they might find it beneficial to identify various types of resources even before they need them. It might also be helpful if they knew not just where those resources were available, but also when and how to access them.

Of equal importance is the need for parents to recognize that ultimately, whatever resources they identify or may choose to utilize, they are helping their children. They should also ensure that they share the information they have with their children's other parent.

A depressed father after his divorce

While looking for resources to help children, parents should also look for resources to help themselves.

Mental health resources should also be on the list. According to the Centers for Disease Control (CDC), suicide rates are up significantly, especially among young people, and about a quarter of all Americans are either anxious or depressed.

A father interacting with his daughter – combing her hair.

A mom and dad being nice to each other after they divorce. They realize this is a necessity for their daughter's benefit.

When parents try hard to be nice to each other after they separate or divorce, it is less confusing for the children. It makes them feel better, and it makes it much easier for them to adjust.

Step #5

Avoid Getting into New Relationships
Too Soon

Getting back in the game after they divorced

Because their marriage was not going well for a long time, some parents are not too surprised when the divorce finally occurs.

Children, however, are sometimes shocked, and they need time to come to terms with the new reality. It is usually helpful when parents bear that in mind before they decide to move on to new relationships. Twelve to eighteen months is usually regarded as a good adjustment period for individuals following divorce.

When individuals meet others in whom they could be interested, they often engage in elaborate "games," which are usually designed primarily to suggest how desirable they are. At the same time, they also go to great lengths to hide the attributes they feel others could view as undesirable.

The reality, however, is that by the time many individuals hit their mid-twenties and thirties, they have already gone through many complicated life situations and relationships that can leave them with significant emotional and other types of scars.

Even under the best circumstances, it can take the average couple more than a year of spending a great deal of time together on a consistent basis before they start to get to know each other well and find out important things about each other. Even so, many individuals learn to wear pleasant-looking disguises that make them seem attractive and desirable. It could take years before the scars that individuals developed in their earlier interactions are detected. Oftentimes, by the time scars are detected, relationships are already at such an advanced stage that decisions to end them can be complicated.

Sadly, for many people, these scars and their failure to disclose them or get help for them cause problems in relationships. Many of these problems surface after individuals have made significant emotional and other investments in relationships and even after they have gotten married. No matter how superficial or unimportant some individuals might feel their scars are, if they are not managed well and if they do not get help for them, they usually surface eventually, and they often make it almost impossible for relationships to survive.

Following divorce, especially when children are involved, many individuals do not have the time to spare that new relationships demand. They have gone through a very traumatic life event, and they need time to recover and rebuild their lives.

Furthermore, although some adults might have been preparing themselves for the divorce for a very long time and may even feel elated when it is finally over, numerous factors, including how parents conduct themselves and the children's ages at the time of the divorce, can result in adjustment difficulties.

Parents could use some of the time they invest in new relationships to help themselves and their children adjust effectively to the loss of their family unit. Despite that, some parents start new relationships too soon, often even before they or their children have begun to adjust well to the losses they have already sustained.

Many children find it very difficult to adjust to a parent's new relationship, especially when they are still trying to come to terms with the implications of losing their nuclear family. What can make things even more complicated is when stepchildren are involved in their parents' new relationships. This usually results in competition for the love of the parent involved, and it can make the adjustment process even more difficult.

Immediately following the separation or divorce, many parents and children find themselves confronted with numerous problems, some of which they could not have anticipated. Some of those problems can be demanding, and they can cause additional stress. Some stressors include supervision concerns when parents have to leave their children with strangers; relocation; missing friends and relatives; financial constraints that often lead to a lowering of the status to which they might have grown accustomed; and having to share their personal space with stepfamilies.

If these types of concerns are not handled well, they can affect parent-child relationships. They could also affect how parents and their children adjust to life after the divorce.

Many of the challenges that parents encounter following divorce can be avoided, or their intensity and duration can be significantly reduced. In order for this to occur, however, parents have to be willing to focus on the two things that really matter the most—their children's well-being and themselves.

Before starting new relationships, parents might find it helpful to ask themselves the following questions:

1. What problems could arise if I got involved in a new relationship now?

2. How might any potential problems that arise in my new relationship affect my life, my children's lives, and our relationship?

3. Will being in a new relationship make adjusting to the divorce easier for me or my children?

4. How will my children view this new relationship, and how might their perceptions of me change as a result of it?

5. What changes can I make at the moment that could make life less stressful for me and my children?

6. If I _____, how will it affect my life?

7. If I _____, how will it affect my children's lives?

8. How will being in a new relationship affect my interactions with my ex-spouse, and how could it influence our ability to co-parent our children effectively?

9. If I get into a new relationship at present, would I be doing what's in my best interest or in the best interest of my children?

The answers to these and other pertinent questions can give some insight into the possible ways in which the decisions that parents make can affect their lives and the lives of their children. They can also prevent parents from making impulsive decisions that could make adjusting to the divorce more difficult for themselves and for their children.

Parents who find they are struggling with making decisions that might not be in their best interest or the best interest of their children may find it beneficial to seek professional help, rather than taking actions that could make an already difficult situation even more complicated.

In order to ensure that they are in a position to help their children effectively, parents should consider getting help for themselves first. Then, if they are still finding it difficult to help their children, they should seek professional assistance for them as well.

It is also helpful for parents to remember that, while they are getting help for themselves, they are still obligated to ensure that their children's basic needs are being met. Parents are morally obligated to continue to care for their children after they decide to divorce, even if they have to make huge sacrifices and experience major inconveniences in order to do so. They should ensure that their children do not feel abandoned while they convince themselves that they need to get their lives back on track quickly.

A major assumption that parents often make following divorce is that because they have accepted the reality of the divorce and are ready to move ahead and explore new relationships, their children must be ready to accept whomever they are in a new relationship with and should be respectful and cheerful toward that other person. If, however, parents attempted to look at their new relationships from their children's perspective, they would probably have a totally different view.

For example, while some parents might find themselves falling helplessly in love with someone new and might even feel they are experiencing a level of happiness they have not felt in a long time—perhaps ever—the feelings are often quite different for the children. Oftentimes, children experience major challenges for a very long time while they try to cope with the loss of their once-stable family.

Furthermore, some children make assumptions about their parents' new relationships that may not be true, and their parents may never imagine how they really feel. They may wrongly assume, for example, that the new person with whom their parent is involved has been in the picture for a longer time than they really have been or that the new person might have even contributed to the divorce in some way. These are assumptions that can lead some children to become unsupportive, and they could even try to sabotage the new relationship in a desperate attempt to get their parents back together.

New relationships demand a great deal of time and attention. This means that when parents get involved in them, there is less time available for their children.

When children perceive that a parent is spending more time with or giving more attention to someone else, they often develop the idea that the new person is more important to the parent than they are. This could cause some children to develop jealous, resentful, and even hateful feelings toward their potential future stepparent.

Parents might find it beneficial to remember that each change to which a child is exposed means that some adjustments will need to be made. While adults might have experienced numerous changes throughout their lives and they might have adjusted to them successfully, children have fewer experiences with change.

Divorce is a major change, even for adults. It often requires major, long-term adjustments. If children have to make other changes following divorce, it means they have to make other new adjustments also. Some of these adjustments can pose numerous problems.

Not having the experience or the skills necessary for them to adjust well to each new change will most certainly affect how well children cope. It will also affect the amount of time they need to move ahead with their lives. Parents should consider these matters when they are thinking about new relationships.

Parents can help their children by limiting changes to only those that are necessary following their divorce. Rather than focusing on new relationships, they might find it more beneficial in the long run to place greater emphasis on their children's welfare and on the challenges they are experiencing as they try to adjust to the divorce.

Other questions parents should consider as they attempt to achieve greater success in their lives and to make their children's lives easier following divorce include the following:

1. What are my current needs as a divorced parent?

2. Do I need to change my job?

3. Do I need to change my career?

4. Do I need to relocate?

5. What obligations do I have in my new role as a divorced parent?

6. What can I do in order to ensure that I fulfill my obligations successfully?

7. Are there things about the divorce that I am still angry about?

8. Do I need counseling to address my concerns?

9. Would I benefit from being in a support group?

10. What other supports do I or my children need?

This is the time for parents to work on these concerns. Getting involved in new relationships too soon after a divorce or not paying enough attention to personal needs and the needs of the children mean that some important concerns might not be addressed appropriately, if at all. Placing them on hold or failing to address them, however, could cause them to resurface at a later time.

In fact, concerns that emerge following divorce and are not addressed immediately can most certainly affect how parents and children adjust to the divorce. Those unattended concerns can also have a negative effect on any new relationships in which a parent might become involved.

The twelve- to eighteen- month waiting period that is often suggested before parents engage in new relationships following a divorce is for a specific reason. It gives parents adequate time to address divorce-related issues that could make their adjustment and their children's adjustment far more difficult.

A man and woman finding love again after they divorced

Step #6

Take Care of Your Physical and Mental Health

A divorced man showing apparent signs of distress.

Some individuals may not show obvious signs of mental illness when they are starting a new relationship. Out of fear of rejection, they may also conceal significant challenges they have been facing for many years.

We live in a society in which there is a tendency to place a great deal of emphasis on romantic love, on physical appearance, and on some very superficial attributes that have little to do with how people really are as individuals. These factors are not good determinants of how desirable individuals might be in relationships.

At the same time, many factors known to be essential to successful relationships, such as excellent mental health, selflessness, empathy, and a caring nature, are often de-emphasized. It should not be too surprising, therefore, that so many individuals do so poorly in relationships.

Many individuals are concerned that historically, our educational institutions have not prepared us for some of the most important roles in life. Hence, when we find ourselves in relationships, we know neither what is really expected of us nor what to do in order to be successful.

Many individuals, some with years of schooling and even advanced degrees, have never taken a course that taught them how to do well in relationships, how to be more loving and caring spouses, how to be good parents, or how to avoid behaviors that could potentially destroy their relationships.

Not enough emphasis has been placed on teaching individuals how to care for others with whom they develop meaningful relationships or even how to care well for themselves. The bottom line is that the inability of individuals to care for themselves and for others is a major factor in the demise of many relationships.

Some individuals attempt to cope with the challenges they face in their lives by engaging in inappropriate behaviors or by using certain means that later prove to be inappropriate. Futile attempts that some individuals make to cope with life's challenges can bring their own consequences, and they can make matters much worse than they needed to be.

There is an abundance of tangible evidence that points to the fact that many Americans need to take better care of themselves. There is also evidence of what happens when we do not. Substance abuse, morbid obesity, poor relationships, excessive stress, and numerous other conditions are viewed by many as symptoms of a society that is not coping well with the challenges of life and one in which its members need to take much better care of themselves.

Many physical and mental health concerns that are common today are preventable or treatable. Yet when those conditions get out of control, they have the potential to cause serious harm and to shorten lives. This is ironic, because our society is also one in which many individuals do try very hard to live better and longer lives. We spend billions annually in this country on health-care-related concerns.

Our failure to take better care of ourselves and of each other is not only affecting our relationships with other adults but also our relationships with our children. Yet, despite what we already know, many individuals do not seem to realize the roles that some of these factors play in destroying their relationships until their relationships end.

Furthermore, it is not until after divorcing that some individuals decide to "get back in the game" and make all kinds of desirable changes in their lives to make them more attractive for new relationships and to give their relationships a better chance to survive.

Interestingly, if many individuals took better care of themselves while they were married or were willing to make some of the changes they made afterward, this might have contributed to improving their lives and saving their relationships.

Taking care of oneself and making desirable changes are important for all individuals at all times, regardless of their marital status. When children are involved, it is even more important because of the parents' role in setting good examples for them. Therefore, when parents take care of themselves during their marriage, they are helping not only themselves, but also their children.

It appears that the high divorce rate will not be going away anytime soon. But even after divorcing, continuing to invest in one's self-care is still crucial. For one thing, regardless of what might have caused the divorce, it has already occurred, and it cannot be reversed. Therefore, focusing on the past is only helpful from two standpoints—figuring out what went wrong and learning from it, which could help prevent future mistakes.

Parents can choose to use what they learned from the past to create a more desirable future. And, because children learn from their parents and model their behaviors as well, they can benefit from the positive behaviors that their parents display when they start taking better care of themselves.

A major fringe benefit of adopting new self-care measures is that many health concerns that parents

119

develop can be alleviated by some of the changes they make. These positive changes could include the following:

1. Consulting with various health-care professionals in order to ensure that their body is functioning well. These professionals should include primary care doctors, mental health professionals, dentists, opticians, urologists, gynecologists, and nutritionists.

2. Getting enough sleep. (Ask a health-care professional how much sleep you need.) Learn to meditate!

3. Developing a good exercise regimen and sticking with it. (Consult your doctor first.)

4. Learning to love yourself. This is a necessary first step if you are going to love others—even your children.

5. Finding creative ways to be good to yourself and especially to your children.

6. Developing a hobby—something that you enjoy.

7. Surrounding yourself with positive people.

8. Reacquainting yourself with old friends and family members.

9. Laughing, or learning to do so, both at yourself and at situations that seem complicated.

10. Stop worrying! Worrying does not change outcomes; it just makes them more complicated.

11. Getting rid of any baggage you may have picked up from the marriage or during the divorce.

12. Getting individual counseling, which could involve both psychotherapy and hypnotherapy. It can do wonders for your mental health.

13. Making sure your religious needs are being met and never underestimating the power of a sound religious belief and of making positive daily affirmations.

14. Giving yourself time to heal.

15. Believing in your own recovery and making a commitment to move ahead with your life. Make sure you take the steps that will help you do so successfully.

After making the changes parents feel could be beneficial in their lives, they might also find it helpful to do whatever they can to maintain a positive mind-set. A positive mind-set is a necessity, especially if parents are to move ahead with their lives successfully while remaining committed to the important roles in which they must continue to function following their divorce.

Man meditating

123

Meditation is a great stress reducer that has many other significant health benefits. Some adults and even some children find significant comfort when they engage in religious activities such as praying and when they use relaxation techniques like yoga and various forms of meditation.

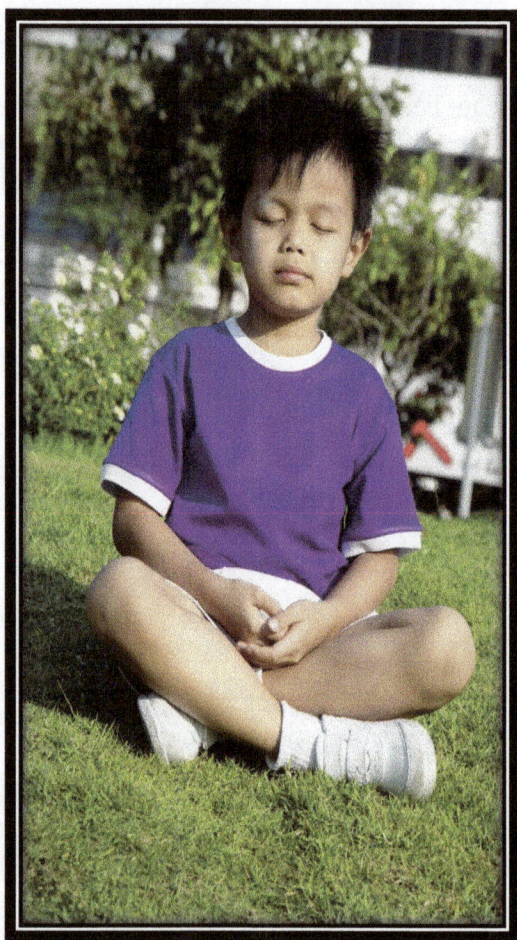

Boy meditating

125

Girl meditating

Even very young children can learn to meditate. Studies affirm that like many adults, children derive numerous and significant benefits from daily meditation practice. It is also very easy to learn.

Step #7

Put Your Children's Needs First

A group of well-adjusted children of divorce

When parents put their children's needs first after a separation or divorce, the children tend to perform much better overall.

While parents are still married, their philosophy regarding child-rearing is usually much different than it is when they are divorced. While married, for example, it is a good idea for parents to put each other's needs first and care for the children and everything else together.

However, many parents, mothers especially, get the wrong idea when they are in relationships. They feel that in order to be considered good mothers, they must always put their children's needs first. So they neglect their husbands and focus on their children, destroying their marriages in the process. This is a huge mistake and a very common factor in divorce.

What parents should try to remember is that they were there together before the children arrived.

128

They both invested heavily in creating and raising them, and they are both needed in their lives. Moreover, if parents are truly interested in a long-term relationship and a permanent family arrangement, they have to make sure that they are both involved continuously, at every step of the way.

Finally, after the children grow older and leave the nest, the parents will be there together again to enjoy and care for each other. Parents should therefore make decisions that will help them put each other's needs first while showing their children how mother-father relationships, and families in general, are supposed to work effectively.

Many actions parents take and many decisions they make affect their children in some way. Therefore, parents might find some wisdom in reflecting on the possible influences that their actions or decisions could have on their children, by asking themselves one very important question: How will this decision or this action affect my life, my children's lives, and our relationships?

By asking themselves this simple question and reflecting on the possible consequences that could arise, many parents could make matters less painful and less traumatic for themselves and their children following their divorce. Yet too often, parents find themselves in difficult situations simply because they acted impulsively. They made decisions that could have long-term consequences without first considering the impact they could have on their lives and the lives of their children.

Parents should be mindful that choosing to marry, deciding to have children, and choosing to end their marriage were all decisions they made. The children played no part in these decisions. Therefore, parents have a moral obligation to help children adjust to the consequences of those decisions.

Following the divorce, while children are still recovering from the loss of their family, if parents try to minimize further losses and the negative impacts many of their actions could have on their children, it can help tremendously with their adjustment. Parents can consult with professionals and use other resources to help them make appropriate decisions or take actions that can be beneficial, especially to their children.

By taking the necessary precautionary steps and keeping their children's welfare in mind at all times, parents can make a very significant difference in their children's lives. Parents should be mindful, also, that the loss of the family structure to which their children have grown accustomed can indeed be very traumatic.

Therefore, parents should constantly seek ways to help their children cope appropriately. They need their parents' help as they go through what is quite often one of the most difficult chapters in their lives—adjusting to their parents' separation or divorce.

Well-adjusted children of divorce.

What does a child who has adjusted well to his or her parents' divorce look like? The answer is not always easy, and it does not necessarily mean that they are always smiling either. It depends on many factors, often including getting them professional assistance.

Many parents will find it beneficial to include the preceding seven steps in a divorce adjustment plan. Others, however, might use different approaches that they feel would meet their needs and the needs of their children more effectively. The bottom line is that parents should know what is best for them and for their children, and they should try to do what they feel might fulfill their unique needs.

During a marriage, although parents have ideas about how they would like to raise their children, they don't often follow a written plan. Both parents live together in the same home, and no matter how imperfect the situation may be, they usually work together to meet their children's needs, or at least they try to do so. All this, however, changes when families break up.

Parents who used to be loving and kind toward each other and who used to care so much for each other and for their children's welfare take on adversarial roles. Sometimes they even forget about how their actions could be affecting their children, and they start working against each other, rather than trying harder to work together for the children's benefit.

The major changes that occur following a traumatic event like a divorce mean that specific and legally binding plans are often necessary in order to guide parents and ensure that the welfare of the minor children remains a priority. Parenting plans can be structured in various ways. Notwithstanding, there are

135

numerous components that should always be present. These essential components serve as a guide for parents regarding their responsibilities and as a reminder of who should perform what functions and when they should perform them.

Parents can consult with legal and child-welfare professionals regarding the essential elements of an effective parenting and time-sharing plan. In many areas, these plans must be in place before any kind of separation or divorce agreement can be legally concluded.

Much of the information covered in this volume results from conversations with both parents and children who have gone through their own divorce experiences and, therefore, know firsthand how challenging the situation can be. The writer, however, does not wish to give the impression that some parents might not already be doing what is in their own best interest and in the best interest of their children.

Divorce can be very difficult. The decision to break up one's family is also one of the most challenging that many parents will ever make. People fell in love with each other, and they had quite different expectations for themselves and for their children than to ever end up in a divided family.

Following divorce, many parents also continue to make extreme sacrifices in their attempts to prevent major disruptions in their children's lives, to help them adjust as best as possible and in as short a time as possible. Despite their efforts, however, many children do face significant difficulties throughout their lives, based on their parents' decisions to end their marriages.

When parents see their children struggling to adjust to significant challenges in their lives that might have resulted directly from a decision that they initiated, it can be very difficult for them. This situation leaves some parents feeling helpless, regretful, and disappointed or even feeling that they have failed in their most important life role.

Even when parents find themselves experiencing such feelings, however, many are still unaware of the steps that they could take that might improve the situation. Against this background, it is my hope that parents might be persuaded to pay attention to the steps that are outlined in this volume. I also hope that many parents will look for other ways in which they can help themselves and their children adjust appropriately following divorce, based on their own unique situations.

This is a very recent volume on divorce. Over the years, however, educators have written extensively on this subject, and much of this information is readily available in other books and on the internet. Whatever methods parents use to obtain information about divorce and how to help themselves and their children after they divorce, I strongly suggest that they become informed before they make their final decisions.

Step #8

Don't Lose Hope

A major mistake that some parents make following a divorce or other significant loss is that they have the tendency to develop a sense of hopelessness about the future. Still, if they took a moment and looked back through their lives, they would find ample evidence of numerous challenges they faced before and how they overcame them successfully.

Many individuals could therefore find it beneficial to recognize that whatever challenging situations they might face before, during, or even after the divorce, with their history of overcoming challenges, they will certainly overcome them as well.

140

Many situations that arise because of a divorce are temporary. And eventually, many individuals do adjust quite well. Many of them have even gone on to marry again, and they are living happily and have great relationships with their children.

After a divorce is usually a good time for individuals to take a retrospective look at their lives to see where things might have gone wrong. They can also identify the lessons they have learned that they can use in other relationships in the future. They can also get the help they need to make their next relationship more successful, rather than having another failed one or choosing to remain alone.

There are many desirable individuals with whom others could relate much better following a divorce. After all, they are now older, hopefully more mature, and also much better informed. People deserve to have a good life. They deserve to be happy. Children might have seen a parent at times when they were not at their best. Now is a great opportunity for that picture to be changed, and it absolutely can be.

This is indeed an opportunity for parents to teach themselves and their children a very valuable lesson about humans' ability to be resilient and to change for the better. By their new actions, parents can demonstrate to themselves and to their children how much they can change their behaviors in positive ways that can be truly beneficial to others.

In order for such a transition to take place, however, parents must be bold and brave, and they must be hopeful. Both parents and children deserve to have an enjoyable life. Children deserve not just to have the parents who created them in their lives, but also the best parents they could ever have.

Finally, when individuals are armed with useful information, they put themselves in positions in which they can make more appropriate decisions. One of the best decisions a parent can make is to ensure that he or she is aware of simple steps that he or she can take to help him or her and his or her children adjust well to a major life-changing loss like divorce.

A father helping his son adjust to changes after the divorce

When both parents remain present and involved in their children's lives, the children are far more likely to continue to do well overall, despite major changes like separation or divorce.

Seven good things a parent can tell a child:

1. "I will always love you."

2. "I think of you daily."

3. "I want you to have a great time when you are with your mom/dad."

4. "You can call me at any time and for any reason."

5. "I will be fine when you are not here with me, so you don't have to worry about me when you leave."

6. "I look forward to spending time with you when you come again."

7. "Tell me what else I can do to make the time we spend together even more special."

Finding interesting activities for children to do following separation or divorce is often a significant challenge for parents.

The following are twelve simple activities that children suggest they enjoy doing alone:

1. Watching TV/a movie
2. Listening to music
3. Playing with a sibling or pet
4. Taking a nap
5. Playing a musical instrument
6. Exercising
7. Calling or texting a friend
8. Calling the other parent
9. Drawing/painting
10. Reading
11. Writing songs/poetry or journaling
12. Playing video games

Following separation or divorce, many parents find it difficult to identify interesting activities that they can do with their children on a consistent basis.

The following ten activities were suggested by children of divorce:

1.   Telling stories of their childhood

2.   Going to a park

3.   Going to the beach

4.   Going shopping

5.   Going to the movies/a play

6.   Visiting family and friends

7.   Playing board games

8.   Cooking or barbecuing

9.   Visiting the library

10.   Building something

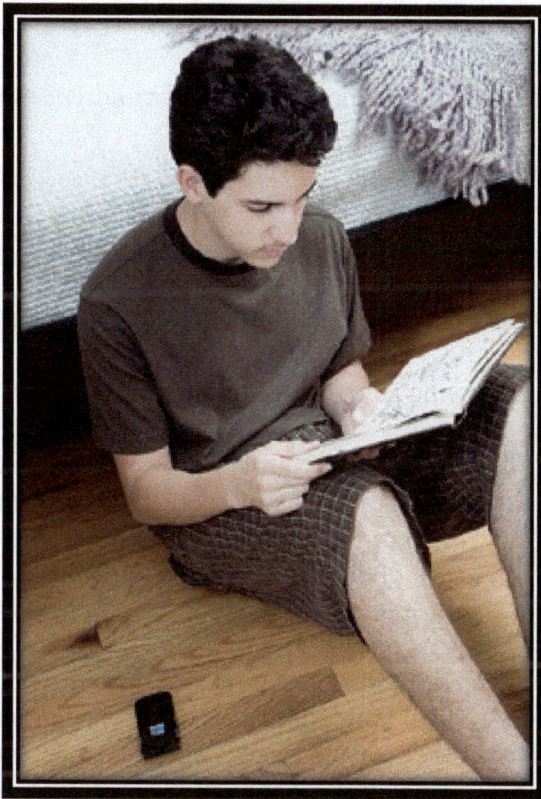

Boy reviewing his journal entries

Journaling is recognized as a very effective therapeutic tool for both adults and children, especially following a life-altering event like divorce.

Merely saying "We are doing our best" is not always good enough. Paying attention to at least some of the following suggestions might help:

1. Know what your child's needs are and make sure they are being met. If you are not aware of what your child's needs are or you are not sure about anything that pertains to child-rearing, you have an obligation to find out.

2. Professionals can be very resourceful. Speak with your child's teacher, pediatrician, or other health-care professional. No one person may have all the answers to your questions, but there is also no shortage of others who are willing to help you find them.

3. Time has taught us that where child-rearing is concerned, some things work well while others do not. Try to familiarize yourself with the things that have been proven to be

beneficial for child-rearing. There is a good chance they will work for your child as well.

4. Try to use approved methods or activities with your child. Minimize or eliminate those that are either questionable or have been proven to be ineffective, negative, or harmful. By doing so, you could save yourself some time and prevent many mistakes.

5. Child-rearing guidelines are available. Get hold of them. Modify them to meet your child's or family's individual needs, but by all means get them and use them.

6. Give guidance, direction, and attention to your child.

7. Know what a healthy child looks like, both physically and mentally. Observe how your child is growing. If something appears to be strange, it's probably worth checking out.

8. Attend to concerns immediately. Not everything goes away with time. In fact, with time, some things get worse.

9. Get professional opinions and get them early. The right professionals can help you

decide whether you need to be concerned or what you may be able to do to remedy a particular situation.

10. Be a positive influence in your child's life and be a good role model. You are your child's first teacher, his or her best teacher, and his or her biggest fan. Set good examples for him or her.

11. Be the parent! Be responsible, loving, kind, caring, affectionate, and patient. But by all means, be the adult in the relationship.

12. Do not "parentify" (discuss adult issues like your personal life and other problems) with your child.

13. Discipline your child and set boundaries. Remember, you are a parent. You are not a friend, a buddy, or a peer.

14. Never abuse or neglect your child. Know what actions constitute abuse and neglect.

15. Be loving, kind, and respectful to your child's other parent. This is the source of fifty percent of who your child is. Even though you are no longer together, show respect for each other.

16. Find ways to prevent your child from thinking that the other parent is less than desirable. If you feel you chose the wrong partner, it's your mistake, not your child's. Just get over it.

17. Never bad-mouth the other parent or put your child in a position in which he or she feels he or she has to take sides. Many powerful lessons on relationships can be learned from the way in which parents interact with and treat each other. If you do not show respect for each other, don't expect your child to have self-respect or to show respect for either of you or for others. Remember, your child learns from you. Also remember that you are not just raising a child. The majority of your child's life may be spent as someone's spouse or parent. You are setting the stage for the type of spouse or parent he or she will become and for his or her happiness as well.

18. Religion has a place in the lives of many people. Religious exposure can help shape morals and values. It is good to give your children some exposure to religious education. However, try not to be dogmatic or fanatical with your religious opinions. Teaching your child that there are many

different peoples and religions in the world and teaching them to be tolerant and respectful of others and their religious views is far more beneficial than giving them the impression that you know what's best or that your religion is best and the only one that matters.

19. Be consistent with your child.

20. Use the three *C*s at all times - Communicate! Communicate! Communicate! That is the only way you are going to get to know your child and what's going on in his or her life.

21. Learn to respect your child's opinion. Listen to him or her. Do not do all the talking. Learning is a two-way street. You may be surprised to know how much you can learn from your child by just listening or observing.

22. Allow your child to know you and trust you.

23. Be approachable.

24. Be honest, dependable, and truthful. You can't be one way and expect the child you raise to be another. It doesn't work.

25. At the first sign of problems, intervene. It may not be just a phase that your child is going through.

26. Get parenting education. Parents can learn from trained professionals and from other parents. Parenting groups can help parents realize that others are going through the same struggles they are. Parents can also learn new ideas and more effective child-rearing techniques from others.

27. Be there physically and emotionally for your child.

28. Take care of your child but take care of yourself also. Eat right, get plenty of sleep, rest, meditate, and exercise. Avoid risky and foolish behaviors. Have an annual physical. Remember: you are valuable to your child, more valuable than the life insurance policy that you are paying for every month to leave a handsome package for him or her.

29. Help is available. Know when and where to get help. Asking for help takes a great deal of courage, but when your children's welfare is at stake, getting help when you can really use it supersedes everything.

30. Allow your children to observe you working hard but also allow them to see you resting and relaxing. Living a balanced life is very important.

31. Be careful what you say in your child's presence. He or she is listening.

32. "Do as I say, not as I do" is not very effective. If you don't want them to do it, perhaps you should not do it. And try not to use the word *don't* when trying to teach your child a lesson. It is much better to tell a child the right thing to do, rather than repeating or reinforcing what you think he or she should not do.

Dad with his daughter after his divorce

Fathers bring a paternal perspective to the

parenting arena that is very different from the maternal

perspective that mothers bring. Children derive

significant benefits from both their parents' maternal

and paternal perspectives. No child should ever be

denied their right to experience them.

References

Baker, Amy J. L. 2007. *Adult Children of Parental Alienation Syndrome*. New York: Norton & Company. http://www.amyjlbaker.com/.

Barnes, M. 2004. *Marriage and Family Therapy*. Argosy University.

Centers for Disease Control and Prevention. 2009. *Parent Training Programs: Insight for Practitioners*. Atlanta: Centers for Disease Control.

Daugherty, Jill, and Casey E. Copen. 2016. "Trends in Attitudes about Marriage, Childbearing, and Sexual Behavior: United States, 2002, 2006–2010, and 2011–2013." *National Health Statistics Report* 92:1–10.

Family and Youth Services Bureau. "Family Violence & Prevention Services." Retrieved from www.acf.hhs.gov/fysb/programs/family-violence-prevention-services.

Florida Department of Children and Families. www.MyFLFamilies.com/.

Florida Statutes (2016). Title XLIII, Chapter 741 § 28.

Florida Statutes (2016). 61.

Matthews, D. W. 1998. *How Divorce Affects Children*. North Carolina Cooperative Extension Service.

Michael, D. 1994. *Child Development*. Fort Lauderdale, FL: Nova Southeastern University.

National Center for Health Statistics. 1997. "Births, Marriages, and Deaths for 1996." *Monthly Vital Statistics Report* 45(12).

National Center for Health Statistics. 1998. "Cohabitation, Marriage and Remarriage in the United States." *Series Report 23(22) 10399 (PHS) 98-1998*.

National Center for Health Statistics. 2016. *National Health Statistics Report No. 92*. Hyattsville, MD: National Center for Health Statistics.

National Fatherhood Initiative. 2015. *Father Facts 7*. Gaithersburg, MD.

Neuman, M. Gary, and Patricia Romanowski. 1998. *Helping Your Kids Cope with Divorce the Sandcastles Way*. New York: Random House.

North Carolina Cooperative Extension Service. 2007. *Long Term Effects of Divorce on Children.* North Carolina.

United States Census Bureau. 2000. Current Population Reports. Retrieved from www.census.gov/cps/.

United States Census Bureau. 2005. Current Population Reports. Retrieved from www.census.gov/cps/.

United States Census Bureau. 2006. Current Population Reports. Retrieved from www.census.gov/cps/.

US Department of Health and Human Services, Administration for Children and Families, Administration on Children, Youth and Families.

United States Department of Health and Human Services/United States National Library of Medicine.

Wallerstein, Judith S., Julia M. Lewis, and Sandra Blakeslee. 2000. *The Unexpected Legacy of Divorce.* New York: Hyperion.

Wallerstein, Judith S., and Sandra Blakeslee. 2003. *What About the Kids?* New York: Hyperion.

www.cdc.gov/nchs/data/ad/ad323

Zamor, Stanley. 2015. Mediation. i-mmediate.com.

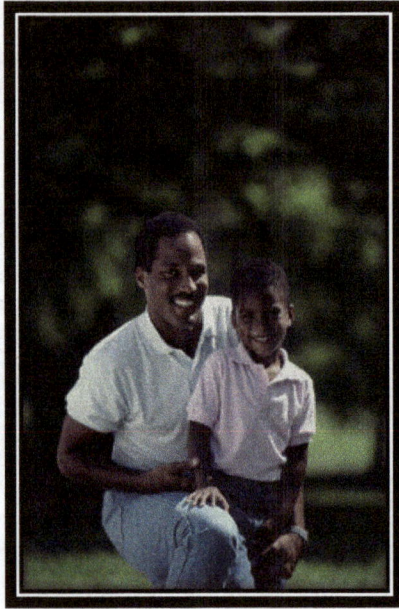

Well-adjusted father with his well-adjusted son after his divorce

Life presents many challenges for both adults and children. Still, regardless of the situation, both parents and children deserve to live enjoyable lives.

161

Hotlines for parents

American Counseling Association   1-800-347-6647

American Psychological Association 1-800-374-2721

Freedom From Fear   1-718-351-1717

Men's Health Network   1-202-543-MHN1

National Abuse & Neglect Hotline   1-800-422-4453

National Domestic Violence Hotline 1-800-799-7233

National Institute of Mental Health 1-301-443-4513

Suicide Prevention Hotline   1-800-273-8255

Victims of Domestic Violence   1-800-355-8547

Useful websites for parents

www.aap.org	American Academy of Pediatrics
www.americanbar.org	American Bar Association
www.coparenting.com	Information on mediation, parenting plans and other divorce-related topics
www.divorce.info	Information on divorce
www.fatherhood.gov	Fatherhood information
www.fatherhood.org	Fatherhood information
www.kidshealth.com	Information on kids' health
www.nami.org	National Alliance for Mental Illness
www.nhsa.org	National Head Start Assn.
www.va.gov	Department of Veterans Affairs

Other resources by the author

1. Grade my parent visits app.

2. *Before You Divorce: 101 Things You Should Know* (Revised Edition 2009)

3. *My Time With My Mom & My Time With My Dad: Guided Journals for Children of Divorce* (sold together)

4. *Before You Get Married: 110 Things You Should Know*

5. *How George Survived His Parents' Divorce: A 12-Year-Old Boy's Story of Fear, Anger, Sadness & Personal Growth*

6. *The Guided Weekly Goal Setter for Teens*

7. *The Guided Weekly Goal Setter for College Students*

8. *The Guided Daily Medical & Mental Health 5-Year Journal*

9. *My Brief 4-Year Journal*

In addition to online bookstores, resources by the author are available at drpercysbooks.com and at cecg2001.com.

Notes

_____

_____

_____

_____

_____

_____

_____

_____

_____

_____

Notes

Notes

Notes

168

Important Contacts

Name:

_____

Tel #:

_____

Email:

_____

Name:

_____

Tel #:

_____

Email:

_____

Important Contacts

Name:

_____

Tel #:

_____

Email:

_____

Name:

_____

Tel #:

_____

Email:

_____

Important Contacts

Name:

_____

Tel #:

_____

Email:

_____

Name:

_____

Tel #:

_____

Email:

_____

Important Contacts

Name:

_____

Tel #:

_____

Email:

_____

Name:

_____

Tel #:

_____

Email:

_____

Important Contacts

Name:

_____

Tel #:

_____

Email:

_____

Name:

_____

Tel #:

_____

Email:

_____

Important Contacts

Name:

_____

Tel #:

_____

Email:

_____

Name:

_____

Tel #:

_____

Email:

_____

Important Contacts

Name:

_____

Tel #:

_____

Email:

_____

Name:

_____

Tel #:

_____

Email:

_____

Important Contacts

Name:

_____

Tel #:

_____

Email:

_____

Name:

_____

Tel #:

_____

Email:

_____

Important Contacts

Name:

_____

Tel #:

_____

Email:

_____

Name:

_____

Tel #:

_____

Email:

_____

Important Contacts

Name:

_____

Tel #:

_____

Email:

_____

Name:

_____

Tel #:

_____

Email:

_____

Important Contacts

Name:

_____

Tel #:

_____

Email:

_____

Name:

_____

Tel #:

_____

Email:

_____

Important Contacts

Name:

_____

Tel #:

_____

Email:

_____

Name:

_____

Tel #:

_____

Email:

_____

Important Contacts

Name:

_____

Tel #:

_____

Email:

_____

Name:

_____

Tel #:

_____

Email:

_____

Important Contacts

Name:

_____

Tel #:

_____

Email:

_____

Name:

_____

Tel #:

_____

Email:

_____

Important Contacts

Name:

_____

Tel #:

_____

Email:

_____

Name:

_____

Tel #:

_____

Email:

_____